RANDY'S
CORNER

DAY BY DAY WITH...

ELI
MANNING

BY
JOE RASEMAS
AND
KATHLEEN TRACY

Mitchell Lane
PUBLISHERS

P.O. Box 196
Hockessin, Delaware 19707
Visit us on the web: www.mitchelllane.com
Comments? email us:
mitchelllane@mitchelllane.com

Copyright © 2012 by Mitchell Lane Publishers. All rights reserved. No part of this book may be reproduced without written permission from the publisher. Printed and bound in the United States of America.

Printing   1   2   3   4   5   6   7   8   9

RANDY'S CORNER

DAY BY DAY WITH . . .

Beyoncé	Miley Cyrus
Dwayne "the Rock" Johnson	Selena Gomez
Eli Manning	Shaun White
Justin Bieber	Taylor Swift
LeBron James	Willow Smith

Library of Congress Cataloging-in-Publication Data applied for

ISBN: 9781584159858
eBook ISBN: 9781612281537

ABOUT THE AUTHORS: Entertainment journalist and children's book author Kathleen Tracy specializes in celebrity biographies. An avid sports fan, she lives in Southern California with her two dogs and African gray parrot.

Joe Rasemas may be writing, designing, and illustrating children's books, but he makes it clear that he is still accepting offers from major sports teams to join their clubs. A sports fan since he first began tossing a ball around with his dad in their backyard, Joe lives with his beautiful wife, Cynthia, and their wonderful son, Jeremy, in Chester County, Pennsylvania.

PLB

DAY BY DAY WITH

ELI MANNING

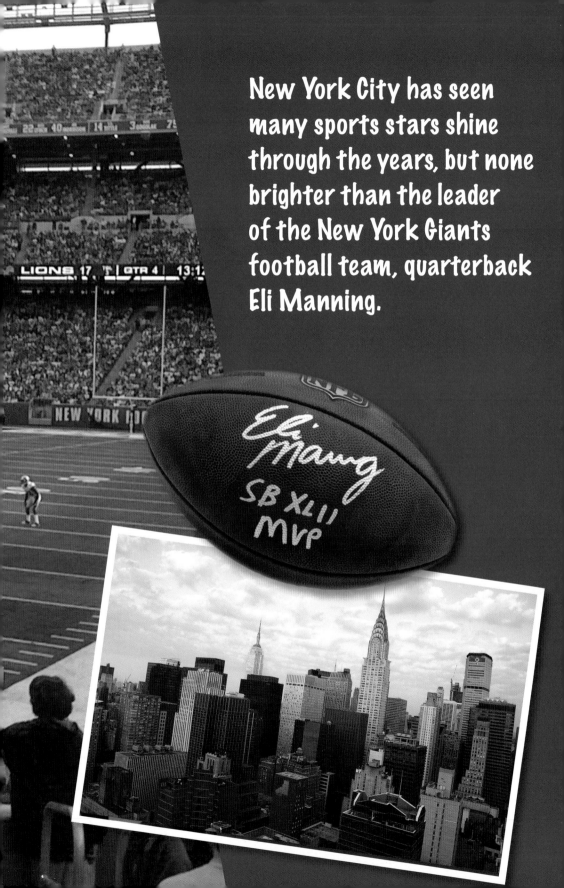

New York City has seen many sports stars shine through the years, but none brighter than the leader of the New York Giants football team, quarterback Eli Manning.

He was born in "The Big Easy," New Orleans, Louisiana. As a young boy, he was nicknamed Easy because of his calm, easygoing style.

FROM LEFT: BROTHERS COOPER, ELI, AND PEYTON MANNING

JACKSON SQUARE IN
NEW ORLEANS

FROM LEFT: OLIVIA, ELI, ARCHIE, PEYTON, AND COOPER

Eli comes from a football family. His father, Archie, was a quarterback for the New Orleans Saints. His brother Peyton is the quarterback for the Indianapolis Colts.

His oldest brother, Cooper, was an all-star wide receiver in high school. But growing up, Eli did not dream of being a big-time football player.

COOPER

PEYTON

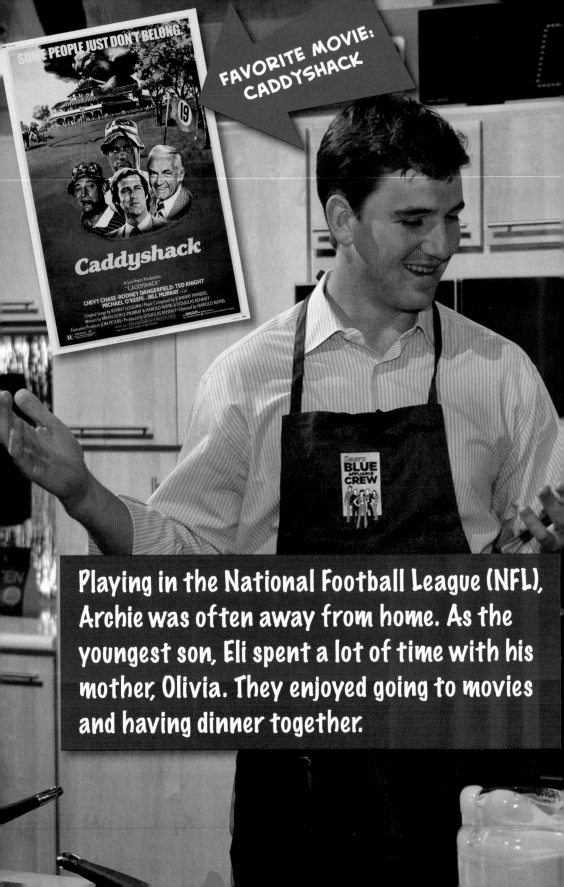

FAVORITE MOVIE: CADDYSHACK

Playing in the National Football League (NFL), Archie was often away from home. As the youngest son, Eli spent a lot of time with his mother, Olivia. They enjoyed going to movies and having dinner together.

At school, Eli sometimes struggled. He had a hard time reading and was falling behind in class. After getting extra help, his reading improved, and so did his grades.

PANCAKE COOKING CONTEST WITH MOM!

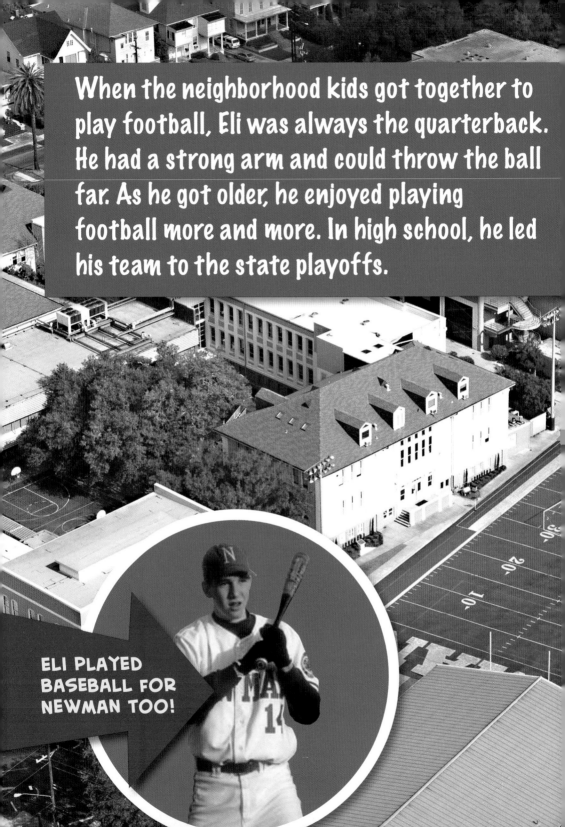

When the neighborhood kids got together to play football, Eli was always the quarterback. He had a strong arm and could throw the ball far. As he got older, he enjoyed playing football more and more. In high school, he led his team to the state playoffs.

ELI PLAYED BASEBALL FOR NEWMAN TOO!

ISIDORE NEWMAN
GREENIES HELMET

Many colleges wanted Eli to play for them. He decided to go to the University of Mississippi. Both his father and his brother Cooper had attended "Ole Miss."

In college, Eli took marketing and businesss classes, went out with friends for pizza, and played football for the Rebels.

As his touchdown passes soared for his team, so did his heart for his college love, Abby McGrew.

In his second year at Ole Miss (2001), Eli became the starting quarterback. He threw 31 touchdown passes and set or tied 17 school records. During his last year there, he won the Maxwell Award, given to the best college player of the year.

THE MAXWELL AWARD

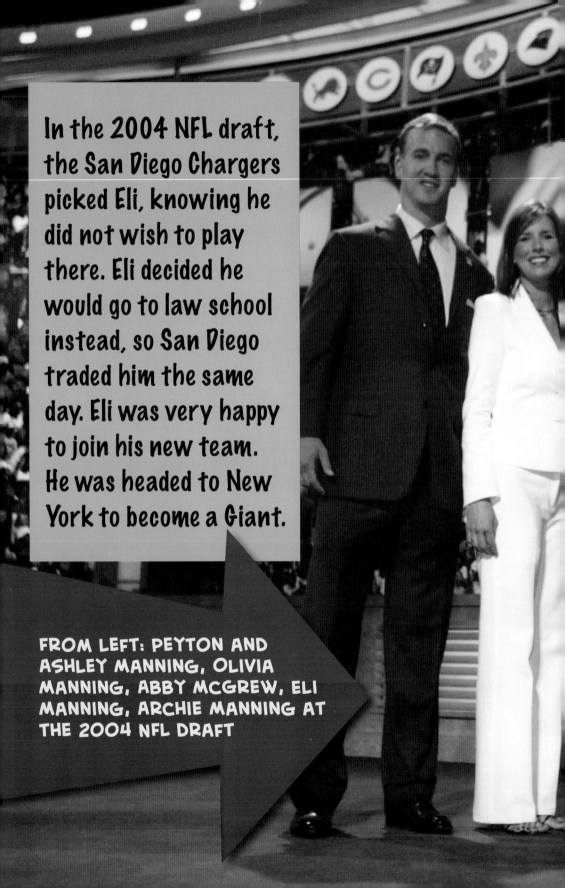

In the 2004 NFL draft, the San Diego Chargers picked Eli, knowing he did not wish to play there. Eli decided he would go to law school instead, so San Diego traded him the same day. Eli was very happy to join his new team. He was headed to New York to become a Giant.

FROM LEFT: PEYTON AND ASHLEY MANNING, OLIVIA MANNING, ABBY MCGREW, ELI MANNING, ARCHIE MANNING AT THE 2004 NFL DRAFT

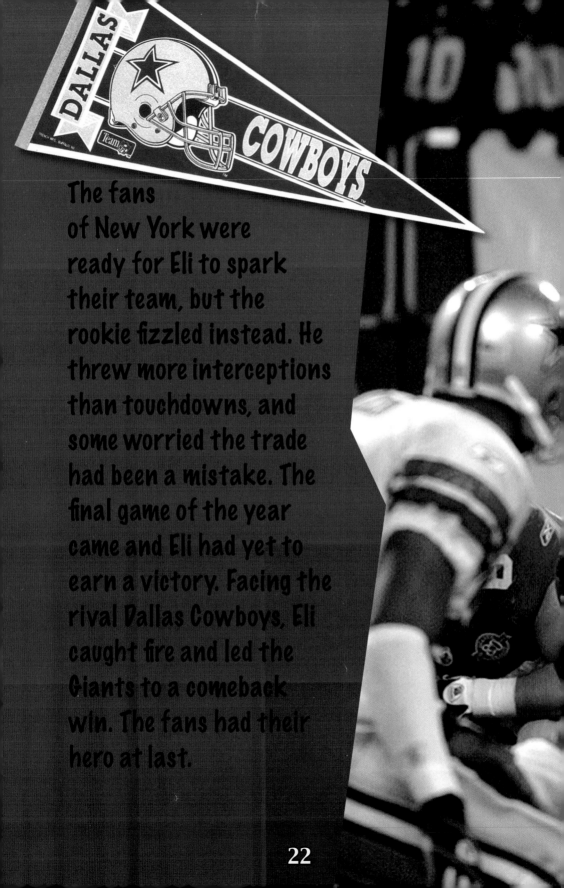

The fans of New York were ready for Eli to spark their team, but the rookie fizzled instead. He threw more interceptions than touchdowns, and some worried the trade had been a mistake. The final game of the year came and Eli had yet to earn a victory. Facing the rival Dallas Cowboys, Eli caught fire and led the Giants to a comeback win. The fans had their hero at last.

The next year saw Eli take the Giants to the postseason, but in his third he took them all the way to the Super Bowl. It was a tense, exciting game against the New England Patriots. The Giants won 17-14 when Eli threw a last-minute touchdown pass. He was named Most Valuable Player, and he and Peyton became the first brothers to quarterback winning Super Bowl teams.

ELI WITH TEAMMATE MICHAEL STRAHAN, WHO HOLDS THE VINCE LOMBARDI TROPHY, GIVEN TO THE WORLD CHAMPION GIANTS, AS THEY PARADE THROUGH NEW YORK CITY

CABO SAN LUCAS
BEACH IN MEXICO

NEW YORK
CITY

In April 2008, Eli married Abby on a beach
in Mexico. Every day, from the windows of
their home in New Jersey, they can see the
New York skyline. Life was good, and it got

THE HAPPY COUPLE

better. In late 2010, Abby and Eli announced they were going to have a baby. Their daughter Ava Frances was born on March 21, 2011.

ELI HELPED CLEAN UP NEW ORLEANS AFTER HURRICANE KATRINA.

Eli has always tried to help others. While in college, he would visit the local elementary school and read to the students. He began raising money for the Eli Manning Children's Clinics in 2007. He also helped launch a fitness program for kids. No matter how busy or famous Eli gets, he believes it is important to make time to help people.

ELI AT ST. VINCENT'S HOSPITAL'S FOOTBALL CLINIC FOR KIDS

A bright future lies ahead for the New York hero. A fresh Super Bowl run for the Giants comes around again, and so does more work for the Children's Clinics.

Best of all, there's little Ava Frances Manning, who may someday follow in her own dad's footsteps in some way, one step at a time and day by day.

FURTHER READING

Books

Christopher, Matt, and Stephanie Peters. *On the Field with . . .Peyton and Eli Manning.* New York: Little, Brown Books for Young Readers, 2008.

Doeden, Matt. *Sports Heroes and Legends.* Minneapolis, MN: Lerner Publishing Group, 2008.

Manning, Peyton, Eli Manning, Archie Manning, and Jim Madsen. *Family Huddle.* New York: Scholastic, 2009.

Sandler, Michael. *Eli Manning and the New York Giants: Super Bowl XLII.* New York: Bearport Publishing, 2008.

Savage, Jeff. *Eli Manning (Amazing Athletes).* Minneapolis, MN: First Avenue Editions, 2009.

Tieck, Sarah. *Eli Manning (Big Buddy Biographies).* Edina, MA: Buddy Books, 2008.

On the Internet

Biography Players: Eli Manning
http://biographyplayers.com/eli-manning-208.html

Eli Manning FAQs
http://www.fantasyfootballchallenge.com/152-27027/eli-manning-faqs.html

Works Consulted

Eli Manning's Charity Work, Events and Causes
http://www.looktothestars.org/celebrity/1052-eli-manning

Lawson, Corrina. "Eli Manning Asks Kids to Get Out Their Pencils and Win Technology for Their Schools." *Wired,* September 18, 2009. http://www.wired.com/geekdad/2009/09/eli-manning-asks-kids-to-get-out-their-pencils-and-win-technology-for-their-schools/

Leon, Anya. "Eli Manning Welcomes Daughter Ava Frances." *People Magazine,* March 25, 2011. http://celebritybabies.people.com/2011/03/25/eli-manning-welcomes-daughter-ava-frances/

New York Giants: Eli Manning
http://www.giants.com/team/player34.html

Piazza, Jo. "Giants' Eli Manning Married in Mexico." *Daily News,* April 20, 2008
http://www.nydailynews.com/gossip/2008/04/19/2008-04-19_giants_eli_manning_married_in_mexico.html

GLOSSARY

interception (in-ter-SEP-shun)—A throw caught by a player on the opposite team.

postseason (pohst-SEE-zun)—The weeks right after the regular season when championship games are played.

quarterback (KWAR-ter-bak)—The offensive player who calls the plays and throws the ball.

receiver (ree-SEE-ver)—A player whose main job is to catch the football.

rookie (RUK-ee)—An athlete's first season on a college or professional team.

Super Bowl (SOO-per BOWL)—The professional football game that determines the champion.

touchdown (TUTCH-down)—A goal in football that is worth six points.

touchdown pass (TUTCH-down PASS)—A throw that is caught in the end zone, scoring six points.

INDEX